Fulton Sheen

Evangelist of the modern age

by
Louise Merrie

*All booklets are published thanks to the
generous support of the members of the
Catholic Truth Society*

CATHOLIC TRUTH SOCIETY
PUBLISHERS TO THE HOLY SEE

Contents

Sheen's true vocation begins

Fulton J. Sheen was born in El Paso, Illinois on May 8, 1895, the oldest of four sons of Delia and Newton Sheen. He was baptized Peter but was called Fulton by his grandparents, and took that as his name. On weekends, Fulton and his brothers were required to do farm work, which he disliked, and it was perhaps those years of doing manual labor that later gave him such empathy for the difficulties workers experience.

Fulton's family life gave him a strong Catholic identity. The Sheens prayed the Rosary together every night and priests came to visit once a week. Fulton became an altar server at age eight, and served at Mass in St Mary's Cathedral in Peoria.

Fulton went to his parish elementary school, St Mary's in Peoria, and graduated as valedictorian from the Spaulding Institute in 1913, a high school run by the Brothers of Mary.

The gifts of writing and speaking

Fulton knew he wanted to be a priest, from the time he was a child, and often prayed that he would have a true vocation. Fulton went to St Viator's College in Bourbonnais, Illinois, and graduated with an A.B. and M.A. While in college, he began to demonstrate the two gifts that were of invaluable assistance in his priesthood: writing and speaking. He wrote for his college newspaper and was a member of the debating team. In his autobiography, *Treasure in Clay*, he spoke of an important decision he made as a young man. Although he knew he had a vocation to the priesthood, he wanted to postpone his formation and study for a Ph.D. After graduating from college, he took an exam and won a scholarship for three years at a university. But when he told Father William J. Bergan, one of his mentors from St Viator's, the priest told him that he should go to a seminary instead. "And if you do it, trust in Him, you will receive a far better university education after you are ordained than before." That is exactly what happened. Fulton received his formation for the priesthood at St Paul's Seminary in St Paul, Minnesota.

Ordination and resolutions

Fulton J. Sheen was ordained to the priesthood on September 20, 1919, at St Mary's Cathedral in Peoria, Illinois. In his autobiography, he mentioned two resolutions he made on the day he was ordained: to offer Mass every Saturday in honor of the Blessed Mother for the intention of his priesthood and to spend a Holy Hour daily before Jesus in the Blessed Sacrament. He kept these resolutions and believed that doing so helped him to remain a faithful priest.

An impressive education

After ordination, Father Sheen continued his education at the Catholic University of America in Washington, D.C., where he received his J.C.B. degree. He then attended the University of Louvain in Belgium where he received a Ph.D. in 1923 and was invited to study for an agrégé in philosophy, (a degree higher than a doctorate); he was the first American to earn an agrege. He also studied theology at the Sorbonne in Paris and the Angelicum and Gregorian in Rome.

St Thomas' influence

The major influence on Father Sheen's philosophy was St Thomas Aquinas. St Thomas' influence can be seen in Father Sheen's emphasis on the importance of truth. Although a scholar, Father Sheen explained the teachings of the Church in a way that was clear and direct, that even people without any background in theology or philosophy could comprehend.

Early ministry in England

Father Sheen's early ministry, during his years of study, included England. In 1925, he taught dogmatic theology at St Edmund's College in Ware. He was asked to be a preacher for the summer conferences at Westminster Cathedral, London in 1925, 1928, and 1931, and also taught at the Catholic Summer School of Cambridge

University in 1930 and 1931. In addition, he spent several summers assisting as a curate at St Patrick's Church in the Soho section of London. While in England, Father Sheen became friends with Monsignor Ronald Knox, the Oxford Chaplain and writer, and he often used Monsignor Knox's translation of the Bible in his books. G.K. Chesterton was a great influence on Father Sheen; he met with Chesterton and asked him to write the introduction to his first book, *God and Intelligence in Modern Philosophy*, (which was his agrégé dissertation).

A small parish

In 1926, Father Sheen was offered teaching positions at Columbia University and Oxford University, but the Bishop of Peoria, to test Father Sheen's obedience, asked him to return to the Diocese. Father Sheen was assigned as curate at St Patrick's Church in Peoria, a small parish in a poor neighborhood. He fulfilled his duties with enthusiasm and increased Mass attendance at the church. After nine months, the Bishop gave his permission for Father Sheen to teach at the Catholic University of America.

Professor, author, and radio presenter

Father Sheen taught at Catholic University of America from the end of 1926 until 1950. He said he loved teaching, and "felt a deep moral obligation to students," spending hours preparing for his classes. Father Sheen began teaching Theology, and two years later, joined the Philosophy Department, where he remained. His classes included: "Modern Idea of God in the Light of St Thomas", "Modern Idea of Religion in the Light of St Thomas", "God and Theology", and,"God and Modern Philosophy". His classes were very popular, and often, people who were not students at the University, would come to hear him speak.

Father Sheen taught two classes a semester and went to New York City every weekend where he gave classes to converts. From the late 1930s through the 1940s, he gave lectures and retreats, and preached at St Patrick's Cathedral and St Paul's Church in New York City. He was a member of the American Catholic Philosophical Society since it began, and became its president in 1941.

He wrote over seventy books

Father Sheen also taught through his writing. He wrote over seventy books, (thirty-seven were written while he was a professor), and numerous articles, including two syndicated newspaper columns. He demonstrated great understanding of the problems of modern society, such as secularization, moral relativism, materialism, and war; these problems are still occurring today and in many ways, have grown worse. He showed readers that solutions could only be found through faith in God and following the teachings of the Church. He emphasized that we must realize we are in need of conversion ourselves before we can do anything to improve society. Most of his books were about Jesus; modern philosophy; the social teachings of the Church; and on conversion and living as a Catholic in one's daily life.

His writing style is poetic and beautiful

Father Sheen's writing style is poetic and beautiful, with frequent use of metaphors, allusions, and emotion. He often quoted poems in his books, radio, addresses and television to illustrate his ideas. "The Hound of Heaven", and "The Kingdom of God" by Francis Thompson, "I see His Blood Upon the Rose" by Joseph Mary Plunket, and "Prayer of a Soldier in France" by Joyce Kilmer were among the poems he quoted most frequently.

The sacramental nature of the universe

Despite Father Sheen's frequent criticism of the errors of contemporary society, his books are nevertheless permeated with a feeling of joy and hope because of his Catholic understanding of the purpose of the world. He often wrote about what he described as the sacramental nature of the universe: that everything should be seen, not literally, but as a symbol, that reflects some aspect of God. He wrote in his book, *The Life of All Living*, "In the broad sense of the term everything in the world is a sacrament in as much as it is a material thing used as a means of spiritual sanctification. Everything is and should be a stepping stone to God. Sunsets should be the means of reminding us of God's beauty as a snowflake should remind us of God's purity." He said that poets and saints have a gift for being able to see the sacramental. "Poets are masters in sacramentalizing Creation for they never take anything in its mere material expression; for them things are symbols of the divine. Saints surpass poets in that gift, for saints see God in everything, or better, see God through everything."

First radio show

Father Sheen's first radio show was a talk during Lent in 1928 for the Paulist Fathers. He became a regular presenter for *The Catholic Hour*, from 1930 until 1952, a radio program sponsored by the National Council of Catholic Men.

Catholic hour programs during World War II

In his *Catholic Hour* programs during World War II, Father Sheen asked listeners to pray a Holy Hour daily for peace. In a talk entitled, "Prayer in War Time," on March 29 1942, he explained that prayer is much more than petition; it is a way of uniting our will to God's Will, and is meant to change the way we live. He said, "Prayer does not so much help our conduct as our conduct tests our prayers. If we think right, we will live right….Prayer then comes before conduct. Live with the God of love, in prayer, and you will act lovingly towards your neighbor. Think with the Christ on His Cross, and you will be charitable to your neighbor."

Titles

In 1934, Father Sheen was given the title of Monsignor and received the honor of being named Papal Chamberlain and Domestic Prelate.

The Society for the Propagation of the Faith

Monsignor Sheen was appointed the National Director of the Society for the Propagation of the Faith in New York City in 1950. This was the perfect assignment for him as he already had a great love for the missions and the poor, and felt called to evangelize. He had been leading people to conversion since his time at the parish in Illinois, and now he would be able to assist missionaries in their work throughout the world. As National Director, he corresponded with missionaries, met with them in his office, and travelled to visit them. He created the World

Mission Rosary, which has beads of different colors to represent all the continents. He started two magazines: *Mission*, a bimonthly publication with photographs, stories of missionaries, and letters by donors, and *World Mission*, a quarterly journal. He always encouraged people to donate generously to the missions and to sacrifice for them. He raised over 100 million dollars for the missions.

As always, prayer came first for him, and he prayed with his staff at the Propagation of the Faith every day. Florence Lee, who worked as his secretary, said in an interview, "He was absolutely wonderful to work for. I couldn't have worked for a kinder, more compassionate person." Sister Marlene Brownette, who once worked at the Society for the Propagation for the Faith, and became a friend of Monsignor Sheen's, shared her memories in an interview for *Faithful Witness*, a CD, produced by the Pontifical Mission Societies in the United States. She said, "He would speak of what a joy it was to see the Church growing in these foreign lands. His own personal suffering was offered for the missions. He prayed for every missionary he met and those he didn't meet." He remained the National Director until 1966.

Auxiliary Bishop for the Archdiocese of New York

On June 11, 1951, Monsignor Sheen was consecrated a bishop at the Church of Saints John and Paul in Rome;

he was appointed an Auxiliary Bishop for the
Archdiocese of New York. He had actually prayed to
become a bishop because he wanted to be a successor to
the Apostles, but he later realized that the office of
Bishop can be very difficult.

Role in conversions

Bishop's Sheen's work with the missions was a
continuation of his ministry of evangelization. He felt a
strong duty to share the good news of Jesus and the
Catholic Church with others and encouraged all Catholics
to evangelize. He wrote in his autobiography, "I have
always had a deep passion for helping others find the
faith." During his lifetime, it is estimated that he helped
convert thousands of people, (through the media as well
as through actually meeting people), although he did not
count the number of converts. He knew that it is God who
converts people and he was grateful to have a role in this
work. He wrote in *Peace of Soul*, "Conversion, first and
foremost, and above all else, is due to Divine Grace, a gift
of God which illuminates our intellect to perceive truths
which we never perceived before and strengthens our will
to follow these truths, even though they demand sacrifices
in the natural order."

Some of his converts were famous, including Clare
Boothe Luce, the congresswoman, writer, ambassador,
and wife of publisher Henry Luce; the violinist, Fritz

Kriesler and his wife; Louis Budenz, the managing editor of the *Daily Worker*, a Communist Party newspaper; Heywood Braun, a journalist; and an actress in London who became a Benedictine nun after her conversion. However, the majority of his converts were ordinary people, from a variety of backgrounds, including his housekeeper, Mrs. Fanny Washington.

He never missed an opportunity to talk with people about the Faith, and was even able to reach people who were anti-Catholic. Florence Lee remembered witnessing Bishop Sheen encourage a woman to find peace through the Sacrament of Penance. "One time as the Bishop was leaving for lunch, a woman came into the reception room to give him a donation. Bishop Sheen took her hand and thanked her, saying she was very good to give to the Missions. She said, 'I'm not good. I haven't been to confession in twenty years. He told her to come to confession that afternoon and said she would be reunited with the Lord that day." The woman did return and made her confession later that day.

Life is Worth Living **television show**

In 1952, Bishop Sheen was asked by the DuMont Network to be a presenter for a half-hour television show. The format of his show, *Life is Worth Living*, was similar to a university class; Bishop Sheen even wrote down his main points on a blackboard (which he said was erased by his angel). He always wrote JMJ for Jesus, Mary and Joseph on the top of the blackboard, which he was taught to do by his kindergarten teacher and continued to do all his life whenever he wrote anything.

Bishop Sheen spent 30 hours preparing for each show and always practiced by giving his talk in Italian and French to friends a few days before filming, as a way to better understand and remember the ideas he would be presenting.

Life is Worth Living was not specifically about Catholicism; it was intended for a general audience, but Bishop Sheen spoke as a representative of the Church, dressed in his Bishop's attire. He presented a great variety of topics including: communism, work, and teenagers, but always from a Catholic point of view. The show became very popular, and viewers sent Bishop Sheen thousands of letters each week, as well as donations for the missions, which totalled millions of dollars. He donated his income from the show to the Society for the Propagation of the Faith.

Bishop Sheen spoke with authority, but also warmth and feeling, and always used humor. He often made fun of himself, especially his inability to draw. At times, he displayed anger over sin and injustice, but he was usually pleasant and friendly. He presented his topics logically and clearly, and was so interested in the ideas himself that he made the audience eager to listen to him and to learn. He ended every show by saying, "God loves you".

He began an episode on tolerance, with some humor. He joked that his angel was receiving other job offers. "But our angel has decided to stay with us; he feel that he could render much greater benefaction to mankind by erasing as quickly as possible my horrible drawings." He then gave the Catholic teaching on the virtue of charity, and said that we must love our neighbors, not merely tolerate them. He said, "Notice that Our Blessed Lord said, '*Love* thy neighbor'. He does not say, '*Like* your neighbor'; He does not say, '*Tolerate* your neighbor.' He also called it a *Commandment*. 'A new Commandment I give.' There is a world of difference between *loving* and *liking*. Liking is in the *emotions*; loving is in the *will*. Liking is not subject completely to our control, but love can be commanded."

In 1955, the show was transferred to the ABC Network. In October 1957, Bishop Sheen decided to end the series so he could devote more time to his work for the missions. In 1966, he hosted another television series, in color with the same format.

Generosity with time and money

Bishop Sheen was very generous. He donated money to build churches in Alabama, had chapels built in North Carolina and Texas, paid to have a maternity hospital built for African-American women in Alabama (during the era of segregation), and gave away money to anyone who asked him. Although he had an elegant home in Washington and chapels in North Carolina and Texas, he was said to be detached from material possessions, and when he moved to New York City, he lived more simply, in a small apartment. He was also known to be generous with his time; despite his extremely busy schedule; (he worked as much as nineteen hours a day), he always took the time to visit with anyone who came to the Propagation of the Faith office. Whenever he would go anywhere, people would stop him, and he would always talk to them.

His nephew, Paul Cunningham, remembers his generosity. "We were walking down the street and it was cold, in the winter, and we were in a median the middle of the street and there's a homeless person there, and he went over to talk to him and the next thing you knew, he was taking his overcoat off and gave it to him." He added, "I never remember him ignoring anyone at any moment...He would never refuse anyone time to speak with them or hear what their problems were, give them advice. It was amazing." (*Faithful Witness*)

Reading

Bishop Sheen was constantly reading; he enjoyed all types of books, except novels. He wrote that G.K. Chesterton was the greatest influence on his writing, and he also admired Hilaire Belloc, C.S. Lewis, and Malcolm Muggeridge. Bishop Sheen was very active and played tennis a few times a week, even in his 70s. Although he was always available to meet with anyone who wanted to talk to him, he usually turned down invitations to social events such as parties.

Problems and difficulties

Throughout his life, Bishop Sheen experienced problems and difficulties like everyone else. For example, early on there were conflicts within the Theology Department at Catholic University which led to his being transferred to the Philosophy Department. He experienced other difficulties, which he chose not to disclose in detail. In his introduction to *Life of Christ*, he referred to "dark and painful hours". In his autobiography, he entitled a chapter, "Things Left Unsaid"; he said that it is better to be silent about any problems he had with other people, so as not to judge, not to feel justified, and to accept that these things came from God.

Devotion to Our Lady

Bishop Sheen had a great devotion to the Blessed Mother. He wrote and spoke about her frequently, prayed the Rosary and Litany of the Blessed Virgin daily, and offered Mass every Saturday in her honor and for her protection of his priesthood. He had a real relationship with her, as a son to his mother. He dedicated all of his books to her, with beautiful sentiments. He said he felt great certainty that Mary loved him and that his devotion to her protected his vow of celibacy. He was consecrated to Mary by his mother when he was baptized, and dedicated himself to her when he received his First Holy Communion at age 12. As bishop, his motto on his coat of arms was "Da per matrem me venire," ("Grant that I may come to Thee through Mary").

Pilgrimages

He made thirty pilgrimages to Lourdes and ten to Fatima. The appearance of Our Lady at Fatima in 1917 when he was 22 years old made a great impression on him and perhaps influenced him to speak against Communism and to love Russia. He spoke of Our Lady's appearance at Fatima in his book *Communism and the Conscience of the West,* and his book on Mary, *The World's First Love,* and devoted one television show of L*ife is Worth Living* to her message.

Three amazing experiences

In his autobiography, he told of amazing experiences during a few of his pilgrimages to Lourdes. While a student at Louvain, he wanted to go to Lourdes, but didn't have enough money to pay for a hotel. He decided to go anyway and to trust that the Blessed Mother would provide a way to pay for his trip. He prayed a Novena and on the ninth evening, while praying at the grotto, an American man asked him if he would accompany his family to Paris the next day and act as their interpreter, as they didn't speak French; the man then offered to pay for Bishop Sheen's hotel bill.

After receiving his agrégé, he went to Lourdes again, and asked the Blessed Mother to give him a sign he would be able to return to her shrine in the future. He asked that a little girl dressed in white, would give him a white rose, before he went to the outer gate of the shrine. A girl, matching this description, did actually give him a white rose when he reached the gate, and he returned to Lourdes many more times.

His third unusual experience occurred just before he began teaching at Catholic University. On the last night of his pilgrimage, he asked the Blessed Mother to give him some suffering or difficulty to help someone's soul. Later, he noticed a young woman following him. She said she was an atheist but felt she should talk to him. He stayed in Lourdes three more days, and he helped the young woman, a former Catholic, return to the Church. It seemed that the Blessed Mother accepted Father Sheen's request for trials and used them to help this woman. He wrote, "It took me three more days to get back to Paris. Though I could speak the language, conductors told me my tickets were inadequate; they put me off the train at odd stops; and it was impossible to find a restaurant or an inn. After seventy-two hours and multiplied inconveniences, sleeplessness and inadequate food and rest, I finally arrived in Paris."

Becoming a victim

He also experienced increased sufferings during his long hospital stay after heart surgery on three of the Blessed Mother's feast days, which he took as a sign of her favor. He wrote in his autobiography, "If I had expressed a love for her as the mother of the Priesthood, why should she not in maternal love, make me more like her Son by forcing me to become a victim?"

Mary will lead people back to Jesus

Bishop Sheen frequently said that Mary will lead people back to Jesus. In *Communism and the Conscience of the*

West, he wrote: "Since the world has lost Christ, it may be that through Mary it will recover Him. When Our Blessed Lord was lost at the age of 12; it was the Blessed Mother who found Him. Now that He has been lost again, it may be through Mary that the world will recover their Savior. Another reason is that Divine Providence has committed to a woman the power of overcoming evil".

Vatican II and pastoral work

One of the great privileges of Bishop Sheen's life was to have been a participant at the Second Vatican Council (1962-1965). He was appointed to the Commission on the Missions by Pope John XXIII in 1962, attended all meetings, and contributed to the writing of the document on the missions. He was appointed to the post-conciliar Commission on the Missions by Pope Paul VI.

During the Council, Bishop Sheen came up with ideas such as including a chapter on women. He had great respect for women and thought they could have a very positive influence on society. He believed that problems in the Church in the years following the Council were not caused by the Council itself, but from the influence of the secular world on the Church. He wrote that there was an increased emphasis on social justice in the 1960s, which was positive, but at the same time, individuals were becoming self-centered, which led to a loss of personal responsibility for sin.

Bishop of Rochester

Bishop Sheen was installed as Bishop of Rochester on December 15, 1966. This was his first experience in pastoral work; he had no previous administrative experience and perhaps was not quite prepared for the challenges ahead. He tried to accomplish many things in a short amount of time, probably because he knew he would be required to retire at age 75. One of his main goals was to implement the ideas of the Second Vatican Council in administering the Diocese.

Bishop Sheen invited the previous Bishop to continue to stay at the Bishop's residence and he lived in an apartment. He began a priests' council. He consecrated two auxiliary Bishops. He offered a lecture series on the Bible at the seminary. He recognized that there might be some men entering the seminary who were not suited for the priesthood because of psychological problems, and implemented psychological testing of all seminarians. He was very ecumenical; he spoke in Protestant churches and in a synagogue, and he hired Protestants to teach at St Bernard's Seminary. He raised the salaries of priests and Catholic School teachers. He appointed an Episcopal Vicar of Urban ministry, and began ministries for the poor in the inner city and in rural areas, and for African-Americans and Hispanics. He started a Housing Foundation, which led to eighteen people being given housing, and which continues to this day.

Controversy

He caused some controversy by offering to donate a parish to the federal government to provide housing for the poor; he failed to consult with the pastor and parishioners and had to withdraw the offer. Some of his decisions were unpopular, and he was often misunderstood and criticized; the local newspapers frequently published negative articles about him. Some thought he became too progressive and others thought he was too conservative, but his ideas remained consistent; he was always theologically orthodox with a great interest in the Church's social teachings.

Bishop Sheen resigned the office of Bishop in 1969, close to the required retirement age of 75. He had some good ideas, which he wasn't able to accomplish, such as buying a page in the local newspaper to publish Catholic news, renting a store in a shopping area to use as a chapel, and buying an ambulance for the poor. He later recalled that the priests and laity made his time as Bishop of Rochester a good experience.

Archbishop of Newport

In 1969, he was named Archbishop of the Titular See of Newport, Wales by Pope Paul VI; in 1976, he was given another honor and title, Assistant at the Pontifical Throne. Archbishop Sheen remained busy during the last ten years of his life, celebrating Mass, administering the sacraments, writing, giving lectures, preaching, and giving retreats. He especially enjoyed giving retreats to priests and felt such work helped him too. He wrote, in

Treasure in Clay, "I really wonder if the priests who made these retreats received as much from me as I did from them". He held his conferences in a chapel in the Presence of Jesus in the Blessed Sacrament and he always recommended priests make a resolution to pray a daily Holy Hour.

Archbishop Sheen was very opposed to abortion and after it was legalized in the United States in 1973, he encouraged people to "spiritually adopt" an unborn baby and to pray for that baby's protection for nine months. He composed this prayer: "Jesus, Mary, Joseph. I love you very much. I beg you to spare the life of the unborn baby that I have spiritually adopted who is in danger of abortion."

His suffering actually helped people

In the last few years of his life, Archbishop Sheen suffered from poor health. He had to have open-heart surgery in July 1977 and received a pacemaker. He endured a long recovery. In September 1978, he had to return to the hospital, where he stayed for four months. He was grateful for the opportunity to suffer as he felt he had not made enough sacrifices in his life. In his autobiography, he spoke of offering up his sufferings to help other patients, and on two occasions during long times of recuperation in the hospital, he was able to see how his suffering actually helped people. Once, while critically ill, he heard that another patient was dying. He wrote, "I remember offering my sufferings at that moment for the salvation of his soul and the souls of priests and religious. I had no strength to lift my hand so I only raised my finger and gave him conditional absolution and at that moment he died." Archbishop Sheen later met the man's wife, who had seen his gesture of absolution, and thanked him.

During another time in the hospital, he visited a man who had survived a suicide attempt. The man was a former Catholic who had lost his faith. Archbishop Sheen wrote, "A few hours later I offered the Holy Eucharist from my bed, heard his confession and gave him his first holy Communion in forty-five years. I had asked the Lord to let my sufferings do some good for some soul and He had answered my prayer."

Shortly after leaving the hospital in January 1979, he gave a talk at the National Prayer Breakfast in Washington, D.C. Accompanied by his doctor and a nurse, he gave the Good Friday sermon at St Agnes Church in New York City that April. Despite worsening health, he continued to celebrate Mass and give sermons at churches in New York, and to instruct converts. He always welcomed visitors and spent time working on his autobiography.

Archbishop Sheen prayed to die on a feast day of the Blessed Mother or on a Saturday (as it is Mary's day), and in the Presence of the Blessed Sacrament. That prayer was granted in a way, as he died on December 9, 1979, at age eighty-four. Although not a feast day, it was on the day of one of Our Lady's appearances in Mexico as Our Lady of Guadalupe, and the day after the Solemnity of the Immaculate Conception of the Blessed Virgin. He was found outside the door of his chapel, where the Blessed Sacrament was kept in the tabernacle. He had celebrated Mass that morning.

Archbishop Fulton J. Sheen can be considered a great priest, not because of his popularity or use of the media, but because he remained faithful to Jesus, and demonstrated real love for others by teaching them the truth, giving generously of his time, money, and himself.

His moral and social ideas

In his books, lectures, radio and television programs, Archbishop Sheen instructed people about the moral and social teachings of the Church, and warned against the errors of modern society, especially moral relativism and a misunderstanding of freedom.

Love

Archbishop Sheen continually taught the importance of practicing the virtue of charity or agape. He said it begins with God's love for us, and our love for Him, and then it must be extended to others so that we will love all people as Jesus commands. This is not an optional teaching, but one we are required to follow if we are to be faithful Catholics. He understood that one of the primary difficulties was due to our feelings. Agape does not involve an emotional response, but is something we can command in our will, and do for love of God.

He warned against the sin of prejudice and said we must treat people of different classes, races, and religions, as friends. He promoted ecumenism between Catholics and Protestants, and Jews. He encouraged Catholics, Protestants, and Jews to be united in prayer, and in charity, but did not want to compromise religious truths in order to achieve a false type of unity among the Christian churches. He didn't try to de-emphasize certain Church teachings to appeal to non-Catholics. He presented the compete truth, and in turn, they respected him for it. He taught that when evangelizing people of non-Christian religions, we should look to what is good and truthful in their religion and begin with that. The majority of the viewers of *Life is Worth Living* were Jews and Protestants, and there were also many non-Catholics who listened to *The Catholic Hour* broadcasts. Most of the letters he received from viewers were very positive and only occasionally did he receive any anti-Catholic letters. He always said that people who are anti-Catholic are that way because of ignorance. In *Seven Words of Jesus and Mary*, he wrote, "They do not really hate the

Church. They hate only what they mistakenly believe to be the Church." He predicted many would change, as St Paul did.

Social Teachings on Freedom and Moral Relativism

Just as agape can have positive effects in society, false ideas can cause chaos. Two areas of modern thought which cause the most harm according to Bishop Sheen were a false definition of freedom and the theory of moral relativism. He taught that there is no true freedom without following Church teachings and the natural law; sin leads to enslavement. He found it ironic that people would reject the authority of the Church and choose to accept the authority of dictators, the political systems of Nazism, communism, and Fascism in Europe, and the authority of public opinion polls and the media in the United States. In *Philosophies at War*, written in 1943, he wrote, "The superstition of relativism tells us there is no distinction between truth and error, right and wrong; everything depends upon one's point of view. All values are relative and depend entirely upon the way people live in any generation. Whatever the majority decides is right, and a Gallup poll is the way to find it out." He wrote in *Moods and Truths*, "In religious matters, if I do not accept the authority of the Church, then I must accept the authority of public opinion."

Archbishop Sheen often wrote about false ideas of freedom. People feel that because they have the ability to do something, they can, and that gives them freedom. But he explained that freedom is connected with truth, and it is a gift from God, as with free will. He taught that only by faithfulness to God can we achieve true freedom: "The freedom to become a saint."

Archbishop Sheen had a great gift of faith; he truly believed in Jesus and that the Church is His mystical Body. Accordingly, he practiced obedience to the authority of the Pope, and doctrines of the Church. Despite his advanced degrees, his fame, and the adulation of the public, which could have led to him thinking that he had superior wisdom and knowledge, he always accepted and taught the Church's teachings with humility. Indeed, he was critical of those who wanted the teachings to change. He said that was similar to how people asked Jesus to come down from the Cross, so they would believe in Him. And, if people did not accept the authority of the Church, then they have to accept the dictatorship of public opinion. He pointed out that as every area of life has laws we must follow, such as health, mathematics, geography, traffic, so there should also be laws in Christianity.

In *The Mystical Body of Christ*, he wrote that the Church doesn't force people to believe in her doctrines, "but once incorporated into His body no one may accept

32

some of the truths and reject others". The worldly are opposed to some teachings because they are contrary to how they want to live. He wrote, "But once it is admitted, thanks to the illuminating grace of God, that Christ is the Son of God, there can be no picking and choosing among the parts of His Gospel...That is why the condition of becoming a Catholic is the total, complete, and absolute submission to the authority of Christ and its prolongation in the Church. A Catholic may be defined as one who made the startling discovery that God knows more than he does."

Archbishop Sheen was very loyal to the Pope and encouraged Catholics to respect the Holy Father. He felt fortunate in having had private audiences with several Popes. He was able to meet Pope Pius XI while a graduate student; he had yearly audiences with Pope Pius XII, and Blessed John XXIII, and nearly every year with Pope Paul VI. He admired Blessed Pope John Paul II and accurately predicted, "I believe that Pope John Paul II will go down in history as one of the great Pontiffs of all time".

Families

The problems Archbishop Sheen described in the 1930s, 1940s, and 1950s sound very much like those of our society today. Archbishop Sheen spoke of widespread divorce, remarriage, the use of birth control, and parents who neglect their children. He said that divorce and remarriage, and birth control are wrong because they violate the natural law. He said such immoral behavior leads to other problems in society. For example, if married couples could break their vows, then why couldn't nations break their treaties? Archbishop Sheen was concerned that parents were trusting the public schools to take on the role of parenting. He wanted parents to see that their families were more important than their careers. He felt there was an overemphasis on financial prosperity in family life and that families must recognize they will have to make sacrifices to help each other. He equated the love of a family with the mystery of the mutual love or the Holy Trinity, and with the sacrifice of Jesus' crucifixion.

Education

Education is one area that even by the 1930s was influenced by relativism. Archbishop Sheen was very critical of the secular education offered by public elementary and high schools, and most private and public colleges and universities. To him, education is not about job training nor learning information- it is intrinsically linked to religious formation. He debated whether most people can even be considered educated; in *Old Errors and New Labels*, he asked, "Can we say that a man is truly educated who is ignorant of the first principle of life and truth and love- which is God?"

Archbishop Sheen argued that education is falsely seen as reflecting the worth of a person- people are judges by their degrees, what university they attended, what their major was- instead of by their faith and character. Like Chesterton, he opposed the idea that ignorance is the source of evil. If people are educated, they will not necessarily be good.

Writing at a time when Catholic colleges and universities were still truly Catholic, Archbishop Sheen noted how many of the secular ones were once founded for religious purposes, but lost their mission. He was very opposed to an education that ignored God. He wrote in *Philosophies at War*, "Neutrality is absolutely impossible in education. By the mere fact that religious and moral training is neglected, a non-religious, non-morality and by consequence an anti-religious and anti-moral ideology will be developed. 'He that is not with me is against me' (Matthew 12:30).

War and practical advice

After experiencing two world wars in just twenty-one years, Archbishop Sheen was very concerned about war and addressed its causes and solution in his books and radio addresses. He believed that the wars between nations reflect the inner turmoil of people's souls and rebellion against God and others. He always said that war begins with conflict within an individual, which then turns into conflict with other people, and it leads to wars between nations. He also thought war could be seen as a result of people's sins and said we ought not to think war is only due to economics or political parties. He felt that sins of hate, prejudice, materialism, and moral relativism, and ignoring God in families, education, and governments all lead to the circumstances that bring about war. People thought that progress and technology would bring unity and peace. In an observation which is very relevant for today, he spoke of how material things lead to divisions between people and how only what is spiritual can unite us. He pointed out that increased ease of communication through technology has not brought people closer together. In *Whence Come Wars*, he wrote, "Radio, telephone, telegraph and aeroplane, have pulled men together spatially, but at a moment when men have lost all common ideals and purposes. The explanation is simple: we have lost the unifying bond of the Spiritual."

Archbishop Sheen warned people not to go to war to maintain society as it was, but to see World War II as a chance to return to God. He did not see peace as an end of the fighting or as a victory for the Allies, but as a complete transformation of society. He felt peace would not last unless people converted and changed the unjust systems, which cause so much division. He thought the Pope had an important role in bringing about peace, as he is the only world leader whose position is entirely spiritual and who can therefore unite the other nations, on a moral and spiritual basis, rather than the material and humanistic reasons which continued to fail.

Peace

Archbishop Sheen explained there are two kinds of peace: an end of conflict and war and inner peace. Without inner peace, there can't be peace between nations, or between groups of people. Inner peace can only come from being united to God. In *Peace of Soul*, he wrote, "Unless souls are saved, nothing is saved. There can be no world peace unless there is soul peace".

Communism

Archbishop Sheen opposed Communism all his life because of its violence, hatred, and persecution of religion. In books such as *Communism and the Conscience of the West, and Liberty, Equality and Fraternity*, he quoted from the Soviet Constitution and other Communist documents to reveal how Communism prohibited the practice of religion, freedom of the press, speech and assembly, and how Communist leaders in the Soviet Union controlled all of the nation's wealth. He opposed the Allies' cooperation with Stalin during World War II. He told Americans that Communism is similar to Fascism and Nazism, as all three are ideologies in which the state controls people, and religious believers are oppressed.

Archbishop Sheen pointed out that only a small number of Russians belonged to the Communist party. He had a great love for the Russian people and felt that if they could overthrow Communism and convert to Christianity, they would be able to offer moral leadership to Western countries someday. He emphasized that no one should hate the Communists themselves. He wrote: "Communism is an ideology and as such is intrinsically wicked, but Communists are persons, made to the image and likeness of God, and therefore, should be subjects of our kindness and charity that we may prove ourselves worthy children of the Heavenly Father. There is no erring soul that cannot attain to the treasures of Redemption." Archbishop Sheen said that Western Europeans and Americans had a responsibility to help end Communism because it is the secular, materialistic, Western culture that helped to create it.

Capitalism

Archbishop Sheen thought that some of society's problems were caused by errors in capitalism. He was concerned that people were regarded as less important than company profits, and that they were entirely dependent upon employers for financial security regardless of working conditions and salary. He understood that the problem of unemployment is not just an economic one; unemployed people feel isolated from others, are concerned they aren't contributing to society, and are not able to use their talents. Archbishop Sheen taught that work has a spiritual meaning as well, which capitalism ignores. We can offer up our work as a prayer, which gives it meaning, and prevents even the most menial jobs from seeming useless to the worker. He offered the teachings of Pope Leo XIII in the encyclical of *Rerum Novarum* as a solution to the problems caused by a monopolisitic form of capitalism. At this time, many Catholics such as G.K. Chesterton and Hilaire Belloc were promoting an economic theory called distributism, based on Pope Leo XIII's encyclical. It called for more widespread ownership of private property, including small farms and businesses. Archbishop Sheen supported this theory and had other innovative ideas to improve workers' lives such as encouraging them to continue their education by attending afternoon and evening classes, and having Catholic, Protestant, and Jewish chaplains in the workplace. (Their salaries would be paid by their church or synagogue). He wanted profit sharing for workers and managers, as it is their hard work, which makes the profits. He also wanted workers to help manage corporations through representation on company boards of directors.

Practical Advice

Archbishop Sheen's advice was very practical and when followed, does make it easier to live as a faithful Catholic and to have inner peace. Much of his advice was centered on developing humility and eliminating pride. For example, he recommend offering up difficulties. In *Preface to Religion*, he wrote, "Circumstances must not control you; you must control circumstances. Do something to them! Even the irritations of life can be made stepping stones to salvation." Pride and selfishness are major obstacles to happiness. Conforming one's life to God's will is what brings joy and peace. He wrote, "You will never be happy if your happiness depends on solely what you want. Change the focus. Get a new center. Will what God wills, and your joy no man shall take from you."

He recommended developing temperance and self-discipline through making small sacrifices each day such as not repeating gossip, and smoking fewer cigarettes.

Archbishop Sheen emphasized that by performing our duties faithfully and for the love of God, we offer praise to Him, which is what all of Creation does. He wrote in *Seven Words of Jesus and Mary*, "The bird praises God by singing, the flower by blooming, the clouds with their rain, the sun with its light, the moon with its reflection, and each of us by the patient resignation to the trials of his state of life."

Probably one reason for Archbishop Sheen's continued popularity is that he offered a positive philosophy of life. He had solutions for the problems people face in their daily lives. He showed us there is another, better way of living. God's love and mercy is for everyone. Our past sins can be forgiven and we can always start over and live in a new way.

Archbishop Sheen constantly challenged people to know themselves, and to become better, not to be complacent or content with mediocrity and doing the minimal in one's spiritual life, but to be saints. The main reason he was successful in reaching people was because he had the same high standards for himself; he was always trying to be a more virtuous Catholic and a holier priest, and was aware that he could do better, which gave him compassion for others.

Psychoanalysis and Confession

Archbishop Sheen was critical of psychoanalysis, which was becoming very popular in the 1930s and 1940s. He was not opposed to psychiatry, and recognized that there was a real need for it; he also said psychoanalysis could be useful for people with mental problems, (although he disagreed with Freud's theories). What concerned him was that people without mental problems were using psychoanalysis as a substitute for religion. He believed that much of people's unhappiness, anxiety, escapism through alcohol and drugs, and conflicts with other people, resulted from a denial of sin and repression of guilt. Many people were consulting analysts instead of turning to God, and if Catholic, receiving His forgiveness in the Sacrament of Penance. He wrote and spoke on these ideas often and when he gave a sermon on psychoanalysis and Confession in 1947, the media published articles attacking him for his views, and creating controversy. In response, he wrote a book, *Peace of Soul*, that explained these ideas in depth.

Archbishop Sheen recognized that modern, secular people were confused, unhappy, and troubled. He wrote, "The modern man is characterized by three alienations; he is divided from himself, from his fellow man, and from his God." If people hate themselves, they will hate others.

"The modern soul which cannot live with itself cannot live with its fellow men. A man who is not at peace with himself will not be at peace with his brother," he wrote. He understood that many modern people were unhappy because they needed God, but didn't know Him. He wrote in *Rainbow of Sorrow*, "Something we must never forget is that every man wants to be happy, but he cannot be happy without God." He said we should assume people are looking for God, even if they don't know it.

There were some psychologists who said that psychoanalysis could replace Confession. Not only is confession a sacrament, which gives grace, but it differs from psychoanalysis in many other ways. Archbishop Sheen explained that in psychoanalysis a person reveals one's mental attitudes; in Confession one asks forgiveness for sins. In psychoanalysis, the therapist asks questions and analyzes the patient (which takes a long time); in Confession, the person briefly acknowledges his or her sins. Patients often become dependent on their psychologists; the priest represents Jesus and when he hears Confessions, it is impersonal and often anonymous. A psychologist can be in a state of sin, but still feel free to give advice. A priest is supposed to be in a state of grace by frequent reception of the Sacrament of Penance, and if he is not, he still has the power to forgive sins, because of God's power. Confession is kept secret; psychologists can write about their cases. Archbishop Sheen explained that a person's sins hurt the other members of the Mystical Body. He wrote in *Peace of Soul*, "And since every sin is an offense against the love of God and brotherhood of Christ, it follows that a representative of that spiritual fellowship should, in God's name, and through God's power, receive the individual back into the fellowship." There is no moral standard with psychoanalysis, and in Confession, we are trying to follow God's teachings. Instead of having one's unconscious analyzed, Archbishop Sheen recommended that people do frequent examinations of conscience daily, to see ourselves as we really are, and learn what sins we need to overcome, but always with trust in God's mercy and love.

He encouraged Catholics to go to Confession often because unconfessed sin can lead to more sin and people can only achieve inner peace by being absolved of their sins. He often reminded people that Jesus' suffering on the Cross was caused by us; we are responsible through our sins. In *The Cross and the Beatitudes*, he wrote, "If we had been less proud, His crown of thorns would have been less piercing; if we had been less avaricious, the nails in the hands would have been less burning; if we had travelled less in the devious ways of sin, His feet would not have been so deeply dug with steel; if our speech had been less biting, His lips would have been less parched; if we had been less sinful, His agony would have been shorter; if we had loved more, He would have been hated less."

The Mystical Body of Christ

The Mystical Body of Christ was a favorite teaching of Archbishop Sheen. He always emphasized that the Church is not an institution or an organization; Jesus is the head of the Church and He continues to do what He did on earth through human members. He wrote in *The Divine Romance* "...Christ Who in His human body taught, governed, and sanctified, now continues to do the same in His Mystical Body, and her teachings are Christ's infallible teachings, her commands, Christ's divine commands; and her sanctified Life, Christ's Divine Life."

Archbishop Sheen repeatedly reminded us that Jesus came into the world to die on the Cross to save us from sin and give us eternal life. He wrote in *The Seven Virtues*, "He came on earth not primarily to preach, but to *redeem*." He wanted us to be grateful for Jesus' great love and to try to live as Our Lord did. He often said that we must take seriously what Jesus said about taking up our cross and following Him; our life on earth is not meant to be perfect, and we will have many difficulties. The only way to salvation is by suffering and sacrifice. In *The Rainbow of Sorrow*, he wrote: "In other words, unless there is a Good Friday in our lives, there will never be an Easter Sunday; unless we die to this world, we shall not live in the next; unless there is the crown of thorns, there will never be the halo of light; unless there is the cross, there will never be an empty tomb; unless we lose our life, we shall not find it; unless we are crucified with Christ, we shall never rise with Christ."

Just as they do today, some people used scandals within the Church to criticize her. But Archbishop Sheen pointed out that from the beginning, the Church's members were imperfect: the Apostles were not all faithful, one betrayed Jesus, some Disciples left who found the teachings too hard. The Church is still holy, even if all the members are not.

Archbishop Sheen wrote that there is great solidarity among members of the Church. The sorrows of the poor, the persecuted, and the sinners are our sorrows; the joys of the devout, the converted, and the saints are our joys. This also leads to our responsibility to evangelize others and to pray and sacrifice for people. We are united through the Communion of Saints with everyone in the Church on earth, in Purgatory, and in Heaven, which is why the saints can help us, and we can help the souls in Purgatory through our prayers. We are especially united to other Catholics through the Eucharist. He stated that when we receive the Blessed Sacrament with the other members of a parish, we are there undivided by race, class, or career, and this unites us with Catholics in other countries in a way that is much stronger than being united by one's nationality. He wrote in *The Mystical Body of Christ*, "The Eucharist, because it starts with brotherhood makes all men equal, because it makes them all infinitely precious as sons of God." He said receiving Holy Communion gives us a greater responsibility to practice our faith and to follow its social teachings.

Priesthood and prayer

Although Archbishop Sheen's work included many different areas: the media, education, administration, evangelization, he said always saw himself as a priest, above all else. He knew his life belonged completely to God. In his autobiography, he said he knew that he could have been a better priest, and was always aware of his faults.

In *The Priest is Not His Own*, Archbishop Sheen asked priests to see that as Jesus chose to be a victim to redeem us, in sharing His priesthood they are also called to the same role; in offering the Sacrifice of the Mass, they offer themselves; they also offer themselves in their ministry to people. He wrote of how the priest is a representative of Christ, not only in the sacraments but in all his work. "When in the confessional a priest says, 'I absolve', it is Christ Who absolves; when at Mass he says, 'This is My Body', it is Christ Who offers His body to the Father; And so on in all the sacraments. But in the priest's other acts, it should be Christ Who is again visiting the sick and instructing those who seek truth."

Archbishop Sheen said a priest's good example is what will lead to increased vocations, not marketing techniques. He also said they have a responsibility to evangelize. He understood that it is difficult to be a priest, and he acknowledged that it was even more difficult for him because of being so well-known. In *The Priest is Not His Own*, he wrote about the problems that can come when a priest becomes famous. "In fact, the more success and prestige we enjoy in the world, the more honors laid on us, the more we must refuse to avail ourselves of worldly rewards and consolations. The temptation to be "of the world" becomes great when a priest has popularity thrust on him because his work calls on him to utilize the mass media, the press, television and radio. Then more than ever must he impress on himself that it is one thing to be popular, another to be influential." He wrote that a priest must strive to strengthen his vocation. "A priest's life spent so much in public must be fortified within with prayer and vigilance: 'Without me you can do nothing (John 17:19)'"His own experience gave him great empathy for other priests in their struggles, and he tried to encourage them. As the Holy Hour helped him to remain faithful and zealous, he recommended that every priest make a daily Holy Hour before Jesus in the Blessed Sacrament.

The Mass

Archbishop Sheen often wrote that we are united by Jesus in the Mass, that the priest offers himself and we are meant at the same time, to offer ourselves to God.

The Mass is "Calvary, renewed, re-enacted, re-presented." In *The Mystical Body of Christ*, he wrote: "The Mass, in other words, is a supratemporal reality, by which the glorified Christ in Heaven prolongs His Sacrifice on the Cross by and through us...The Mass is the tremendous experience of Golgotha with its forgiveness and its love, its power and its pardon extended and prolonged even unto this hour." He advised us that when we receive the Holy Communion, we should not receive Jesus passively, but give of ourselves too. In *Calvary and the Mass*, he wrote: "We give Him our time; He gives us His eternity. We give Him our humanity; He gives us His divinity. We give Him our nothingness; He gives us His All." He added that we should live differently because of participating at Mass. "His sacrifice is made our sacrifice by making it the oblation of ourselves in union with Him; His life given for us becomes our life given for Him. Thus do we return from Mass as those who have made their choice, turned their backs upon the world, and become for the generation in which we live other Christs- living potent witnesses to the Love that died that we might live with Love."

Prayer

He frequently warned of the danger of substituting action for prayer. He wanted everyone to do the works of mercy, but emphasized that prayer must come first. This was how he lived, and he still had enough time to accomplish many things. Archbishop Sheen's main priority every day was prayer. He began each morning with a Holy Hour before the Blessed Sacrament; he celebrated Mass, and prayed for others. In every place he lived, he had a room made into a chapel, and was always able to live with Jesus' Presence in the Blessed Sacrament in his home. Monsignor Hilary Franco, who lived and worked with Archbishop Sheen during his time at the Society for the Propagation of the Faith, remembered that when he got up at 6:00 am on his first morning at the apartment, he opened the door to the chapel and saw Archbishop Sheen. "There he was, kneeling in front of his Lord, at that early time", Monsignor Franco said in *Faithful Witness*. Even when travelling, Archbishop Sheen never missed praying the Holy Hour. He depended on that time with Jesus to protect his vocation and to give him the strength for all his work for souls. He recommended this devotion to everyone and especially to priests as they face so many trials and challenges; he believed this was the most powerful way to pray. In *God Love You*, Archbishop Sheen defined prayer in this way: "Prayer is the lifting up of our hearts and minds to God. More simply still, it is communion with God."

Cause for canonization

Archbishop Sheen gave such good example during his life that many people were convinced of his sanctity. The Congregation for the Causes of Saints began the process for his cause on September 14, 2002 and he received the title, Servant of God. On September 29, 2003, the Diocesan Tribunal of Inquiry began in Peoria, Illinois (the Diocese where Sheen was ordained a priest), and documents on two miraculous healings through his intercession were submitted in Rome. The Diocesan phase was concluded in February 2008, and the cause for his beatification and canonization was officially opened in Rome in April 2008. Much progress has been made and in May of 2011, Bishop Daniel Jenky, CSC, of Peoria presented the *positio* to Pope Benedict XVI. The *positio* gives examples of his heroic virtue and his accomplishments.

The Congregation for the Causes of Saints is investigating the healing of a baby through Archbishop's Sheen's intercession as a possible miracle. In September 2010, a baby boy was born stillborn and was without a pulse for 61 minutes. His mother immediately prayed for the Archbishop's help; she had already been asking for his intercession during her pregnancy and had named her son James Fulton. The baby lived but the doctors were uncertain of his progress. The parents had a Mass and Holy Hour offered for their son's healing at St Mary's Cathedral in Peoria and people who heard about James Fulton prayed for Archbishop Sheen's intercessions. The baby completely recovered and is now over a year old. The Congregation for Saints Causes is also investigating the healing of a seventy-two year old woman who experienced serious complications from lung surgery and whose husband prayed for Archbishop Sheen's help.

Archbishop Sheen's vice-postulator, Father Andrew Apostoli, CFR, first met Sheen while a Capuchin brother in Geneva, New York in December 1966. He asked Sheen if he would ordain him the following spring, and he said he would. As usual, Archbishop Sheen was extremely busy but still was able to keep his promise. He ordained Father Apostoli on March 16, 1967. Today, Father Apostoli, who became one of the founders of the Franciscan Friars of the Renewal, has a similar ministry to Archbishop Sheen: writing books, giving talks, and presenting television shows. He remembered that Sheen said in his homily at his ordination: "If there is any key to the reform of the Church, and to the salvation of the world, it lies in the renewal of the priesthood. Become with me, the beginning of a sanctified priesthood." He said, "I want to see him canonized because we can't let his voice and message go silent in the Catholic Church. His canonization would give his works an official approval by the Church of his teachings. His books, his tapes, his television shows are having a positive influence. His teachings are very important."

Two months before he died, Archbishop Sheen was warmly greeted by Pope John Paul II during his visit to St Patrick's Cathedral in New York. The Holy Father embraced him and said, "You have written and spoken well of the Lord Jesus! You have been a loyal son of The Church."

54

Bibliography

www.archbishopsheencause.org

Works about Archbishop Sheen

Connor, Charles P. *The Spiritual Legacy of Archbishop Fulton J. Sheen*. Staten Island, New York: Society of St Paul, Alba House, 2010.

Faithful Witness: The Life and Legacy of Archbishop Fulton J. Sheen. Pontifical Mission Societies in the United States, 2009. (Compact Disc).

Riley, Kathleen L. *Fulton J. Sheen: An American Catholic Response to the Twentieth Century*. Staten Island, New York: Society of St Paul, 2004.

Reeves, Thomas C. *America's Bishop: The Life and Times of Fulton J. Sheen*. San Francisco, CA: Encounter Books, 2002.

Works by Archbishop Sheen

Calvary and the Mass. New York: P.J. Kennedy and Sons, 1936.

Communism and the Conscience of the West. New York: The Bobbs-Merrill Co., l948.

God Love You. Garden City, New York: 1981.

Life is Worth Living, Second Series. New York: McGraw-Hill Book Co., 1954.

Moods and Truths. New York: The Century Co., l932.

Old Errors and New Labels. New York: Appleton-Century Co., 1935.

Peace. Huntington, IN: Our Sunday Visitor, l942.

Peace of Soul. New York: Whittlesey House, l947.

Philosophies at War. New York: Charles Scribner's Sons, 1943.

Preface to Religion. New York: P.J. Kennedy and Sons, 1946.

Rainbow of Sorrow. New York: P.J. Kennedy and Sons, 1938.

Seven Words of Jesus and Mary. New York: P.J. Kennedy and Sons, 1945.

The Cross and the Beatitudes. New York: P.J. Kennedy and Sons, 1937.

The Divine Romance. New York: The Century Co., 1930.

The Life of All Living: The Philosophy of Life. Garden City, New York: Garden City Books, 1951.

The Life of Christ. New York: McGraw-Hill Book Co., l958.

The Mystical Body of Christ. New York: Sheed and Ward, 1935.

The Priest Is Not His Own. New York: McGraw-Hill Book Co., 1963.

The Seven Virtues. New York: P.J. Kennedy and Sons, 1940.

Treasure in Clay. Garden City, New York: Doubleday, 1980.

Whence Come Wars. New York: Sheed and Ward, 1940.

A world of Catholic reading at your fingertips...

Catholic Faith, Life & Truth for all

www.cts-online.org.uk

ctscatholiccompass.org

twitter: @CTSpublishers

facebook.com/CTSpublishers

Catholic Truth Society, Publishers to the Holy See.